W9-CGO-994

The Best of

AC/DC

Cover photograph by George Bodnar
Transcriptions by Ralph Agresta
Edited by Askold Buk

Order No. AM 76688
US ISBN 0.8256.2582.3
UK ISBN 0.7119.1975.5

Exclusive Distributors:
Music Sales Corporation
257 Park Avenue South, New York, New York 10010 USA
Music Sales Limited
8/9 Frith Street, London W1V 5TZ England
Music Sales Pty. Limited
120 Rothschild Street, Rosebery, Sydney, NSW 2018, Australia

Printed in the United States of America by
Vicks Lithograph and Printing Corporation

Amsco Publications
New York/London/Sydney/Cologne

Legend of Musical Symbols

Highway To Hell

Ronald Scott/Angus Young/Malcolm Young

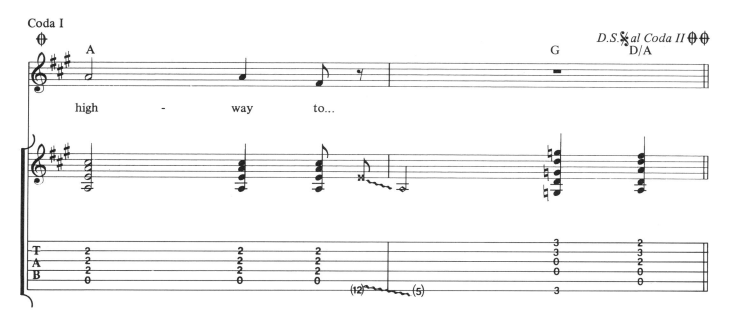

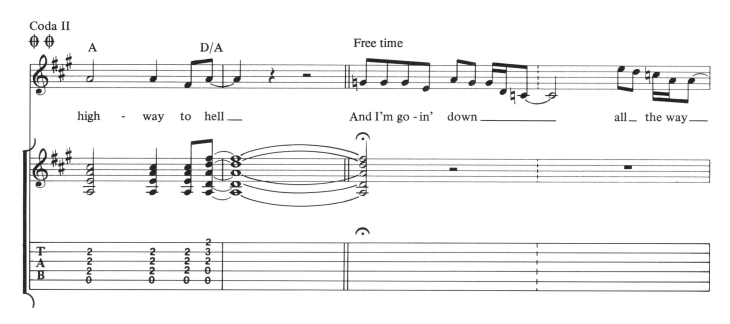

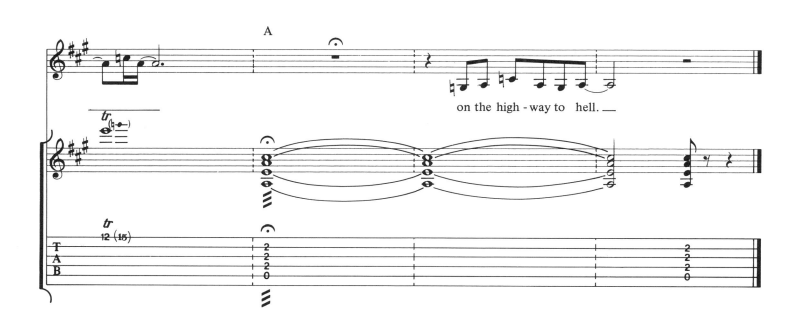

You Shook Me All Night Long

Angus Young/Malcolm Young/Brian Johnson

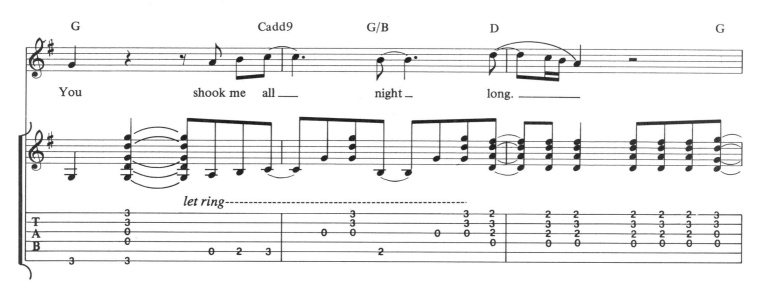

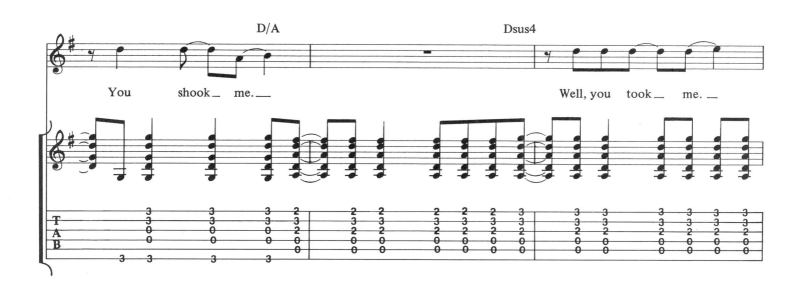

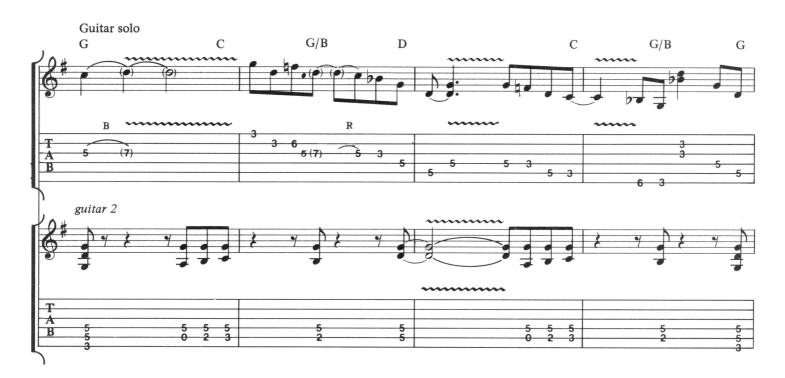

Let's Get It Up

Angus Young/Malcolm Young/Brian Johnson

ad lib solo (16 bars)

Additional Lyrics

2. Loose wires cause fires,
   Gettin' tangled in my desires.
   So screw 'em up, plug 'em in,
   Then switch it on and start all over again.
   I'm gonna get it up.
   Never gonna let it up.
   Tickin' like a time bomb,
   Blowin' out the fuse box.
   Never go down, so

Back In Black

Angus Young/Malcolm Young/Brian Johnson

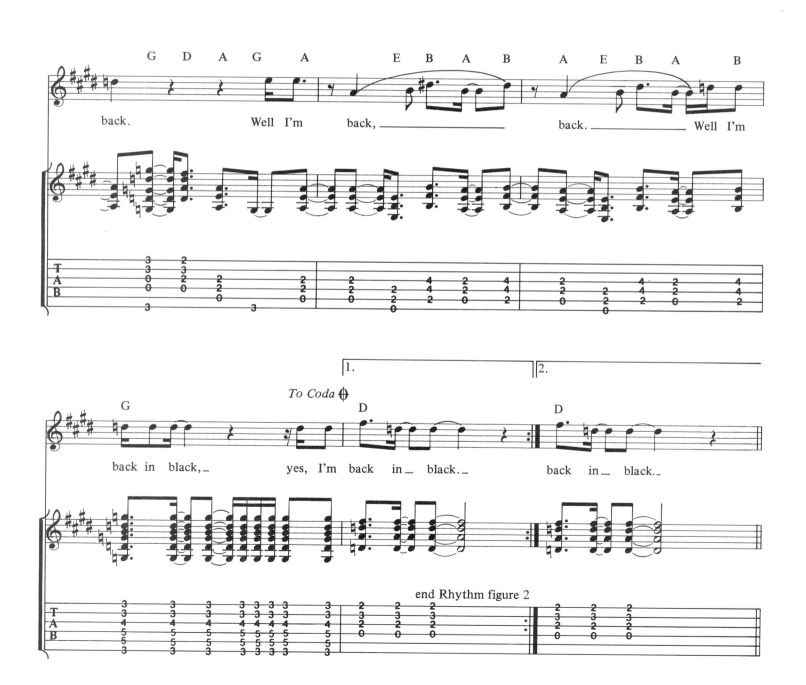

back in___ black.___

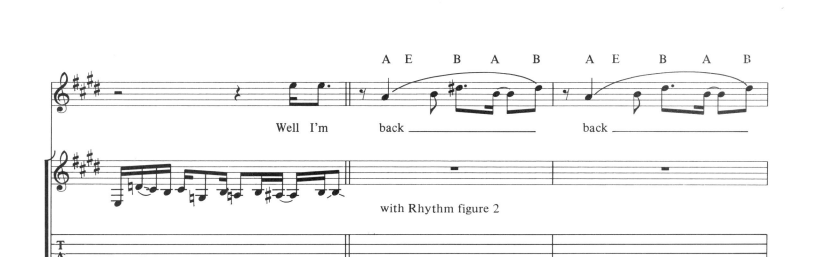

Well I'm   back _____   back _____

with Rhythm figure 2

Additional Lyrics

2. Back in the back of a Cadillac
Number one with a bullet, I'm a power pack.
Yes, I'm in a bang with the gang,
They gotta catch me if they want me to hang.
'Cause I'm back on the track, and I'm beatin' the flack
Nobody's gonna get me on another rap.
So, look at me now, I'm just makin' my play
Don't try to push your luck, just get outta my way.

Heatseeker

Malcolm Young/Angus Young/Brian Johnson

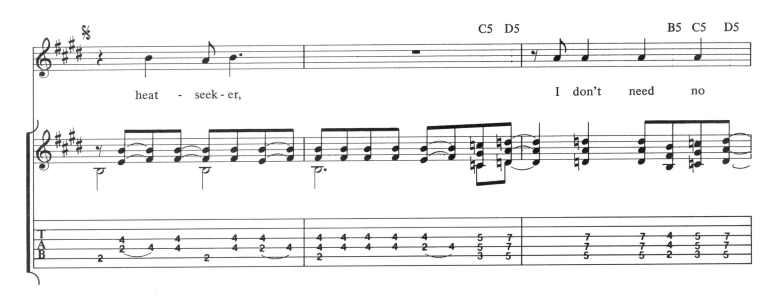

heat - seek - er,   I don't need no

life pre - serv - er.   I don't need no one to hose_ me_ down,_

with Rhythm figure 1

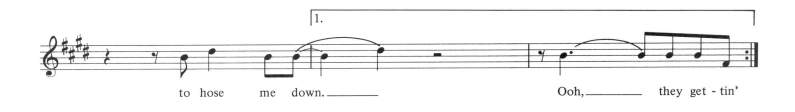

to hose me down._____   Ooh,_____ they get - tin'

with Rhythm figure 1 (first 3 bars)

Ah, you got it.

Hells Bells

Angus Young/Malcolm Young/Brian Johnson

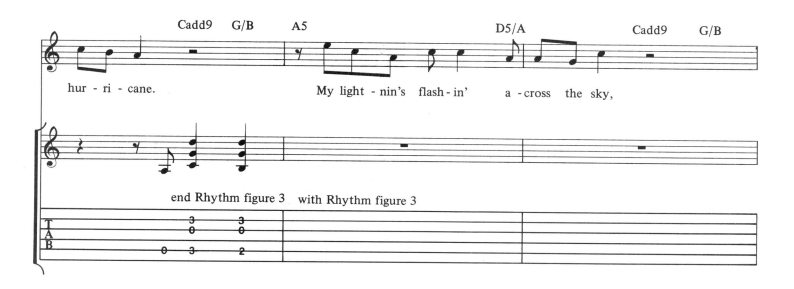

hur - ri - cane.   My light - nin's flash - in'   a - cross the sky,

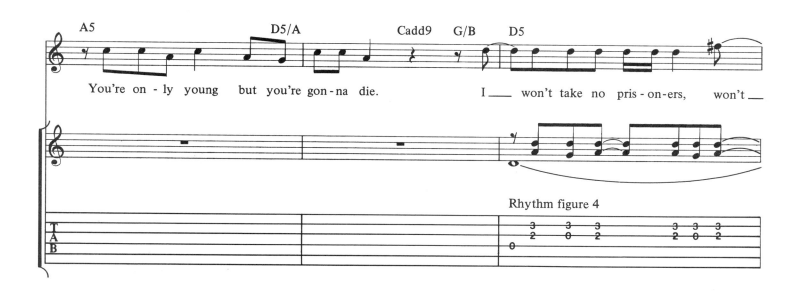

You're on - ly young   but you're gon - na die.   I __ won't take no pris - on - ers,   won't __

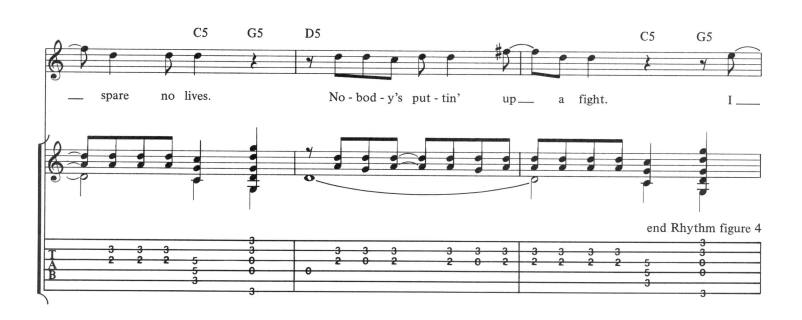

__ spare   no lives.   No - bod - y's put - tin'   up __ a fight.   I __

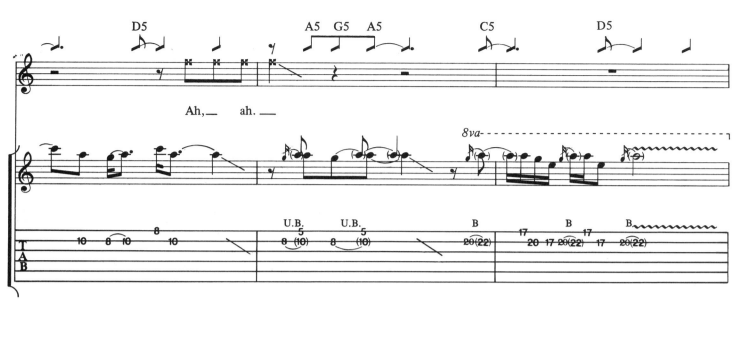

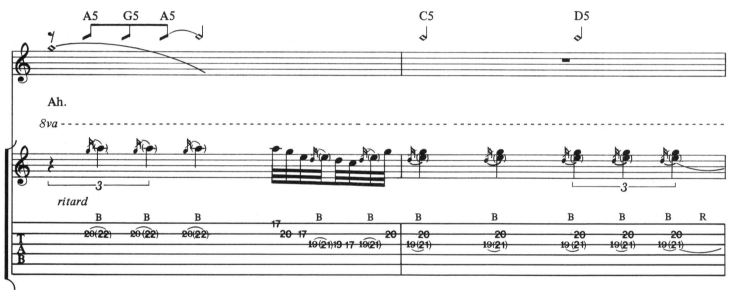

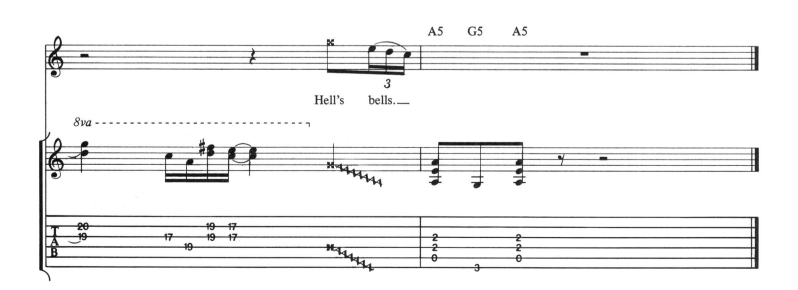

Hell Ain't Such A Bad Place To Be

Ronald Scott/Angus Young/Malcolm Young

play 4 times

Rhythm figure 1

end Rhythm figure 1

with Rhythm figure 1 (4 times)

Some-

-times I think this wom-an is kind-a hot,

Some-

-times I think this wom-an is some-times not.

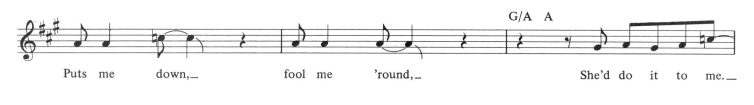

Puts me down,___ fool me 'round,___ She'd do it to me.___

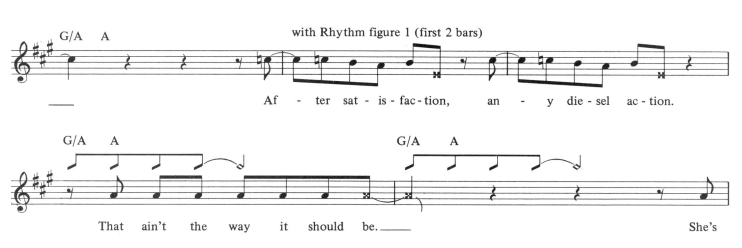

___ Af - ter sat - is - fac - tion, an - y die - sel ac - tion.

That ain't the way it should be.___ She's

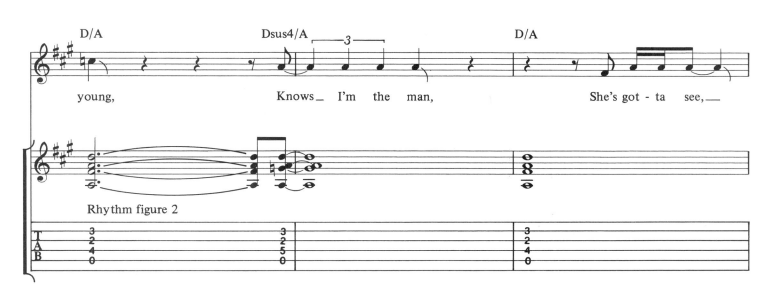

young, Knows___ I'm the man, She's got - ta see,___

Rhythm figure 2

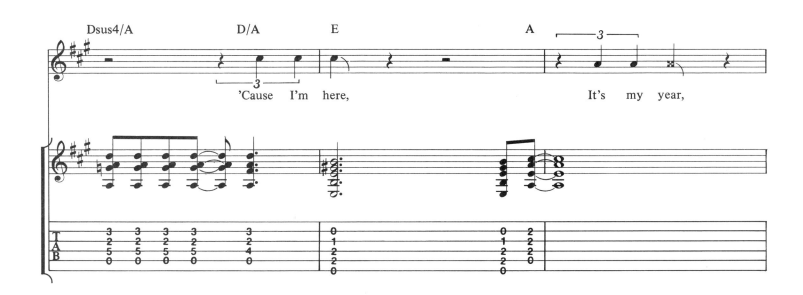

'Cause I'm here, It's my year,

42

43

Problem Child

Bon Scott/Malcolm Young/Angus Young

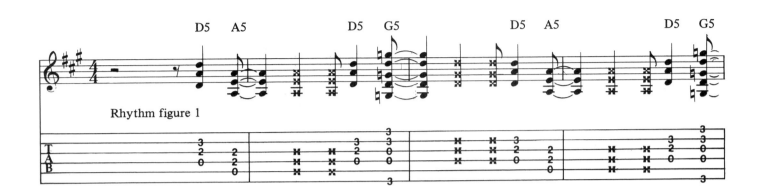

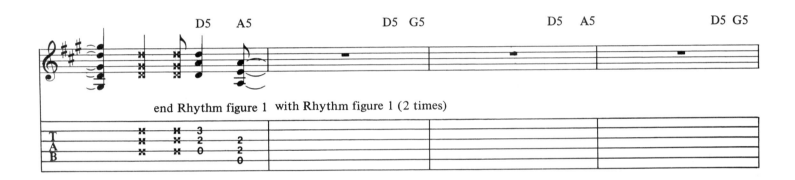

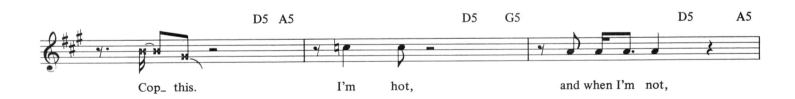

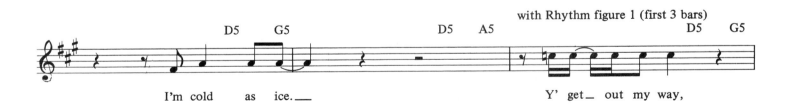

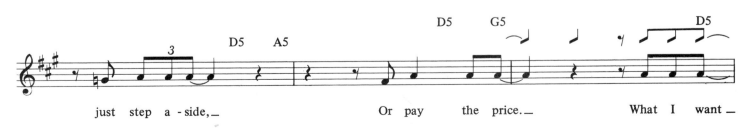

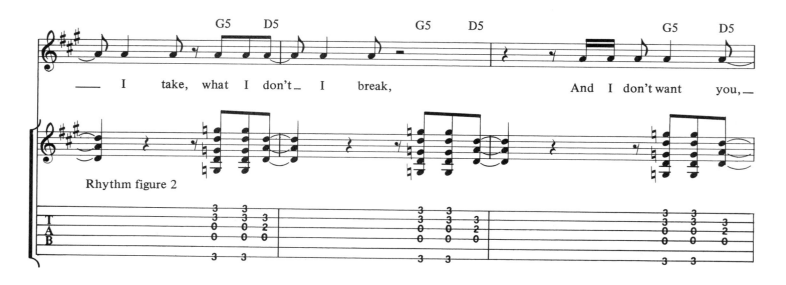

I take, what I don't_ I break, And I don't want you,_

Rhythm figure 2

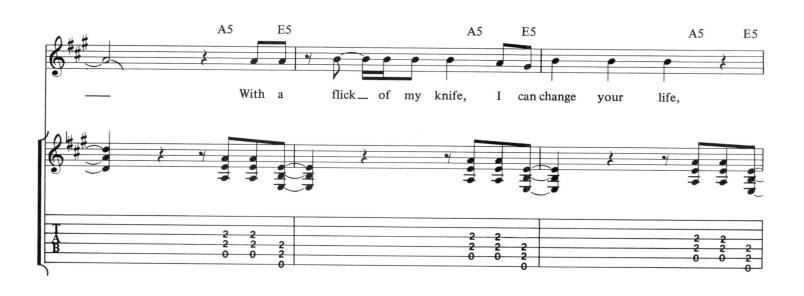

_ With a flick_ of my knife, I can change your life,

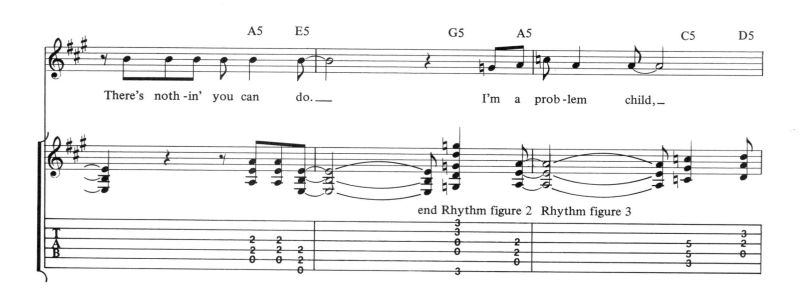

There's noth-in' you can do._ I'm a prob-lem child,_

end Rhythm figure 2   Rhythm figure 3

with Rhythm figure 3

Just watch your step.

Ev'-ry night, street a-light,— I drink my booze,

Touch Too Much

Ronald Scott/Malcolm Young/Angus Young

Who Made Who

Angus Young/Malcolm Young/Brian Johnson

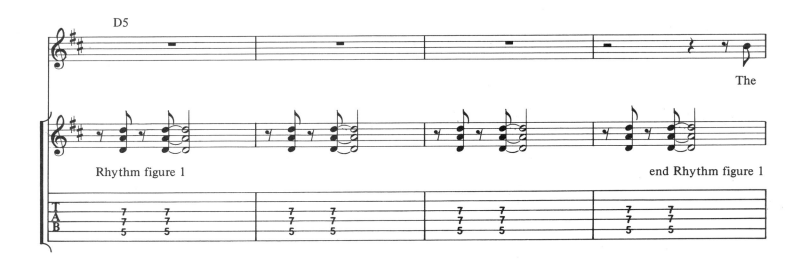

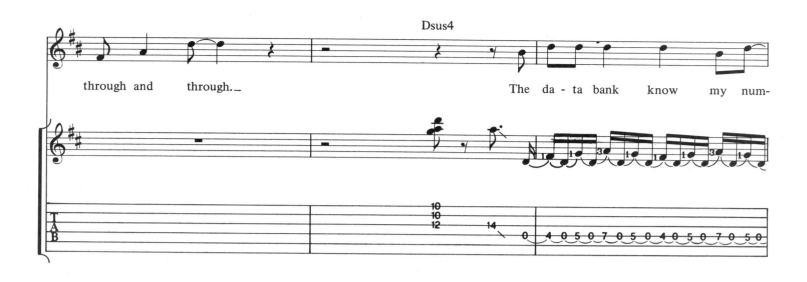

through and through.___ The da-ta bank know my num-

-ber. Says I got-ta pay 'cause I

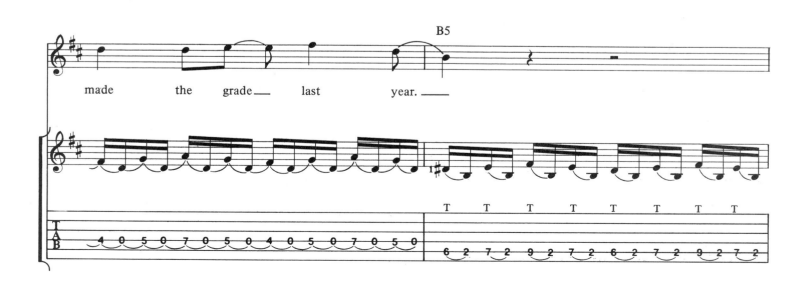

made the grade___ last year. ___

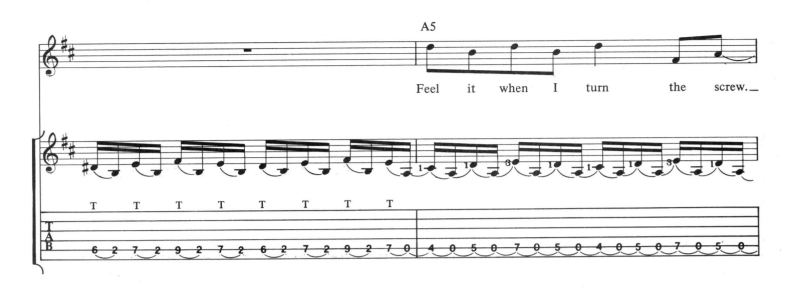

Feel it when I turn the screw. ___

___ Kick you 'round the world. There ain't ___

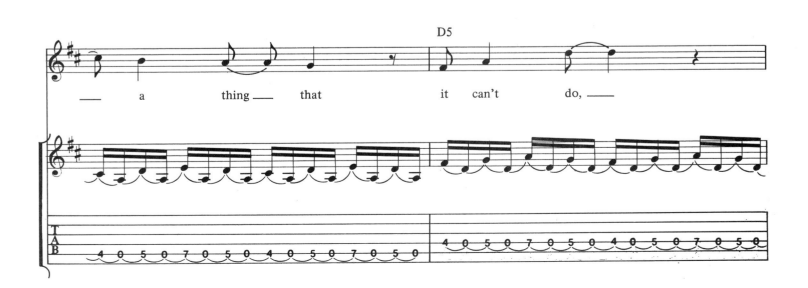

___ a thing ___ that it can't do, ___

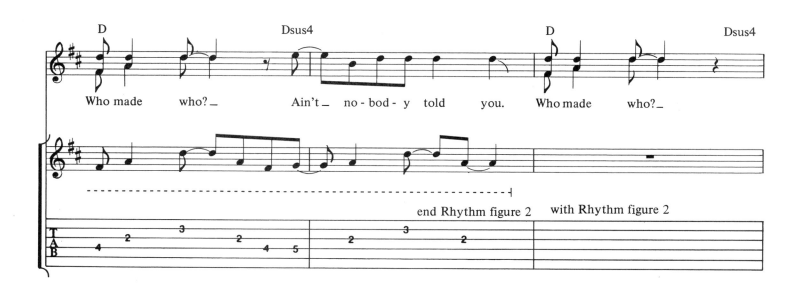

To Coda ⊕

Who made you?_ If you made them and they_ made you, Who pick up_ the mid - dle and who_ made_

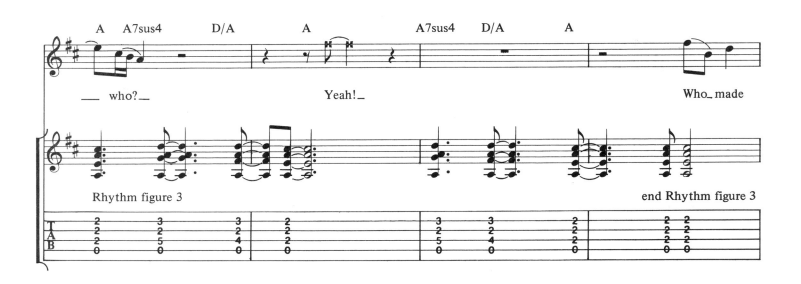

_ who?_ Yeah!_ Who_ made

Rhythm figure 3

end Rhythm figure 3

with Rhythm figure 2

who? Who_ turned the screw?

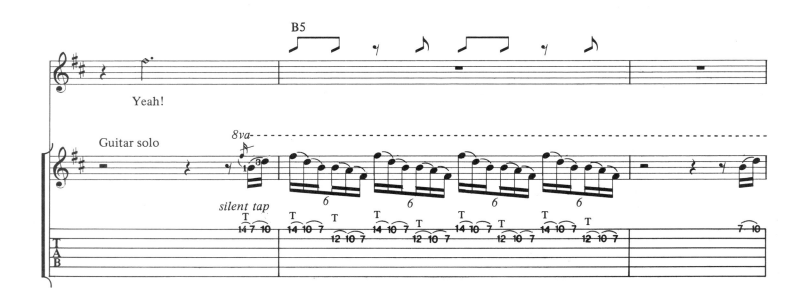

Yeah!

Guitar solo

silent tap

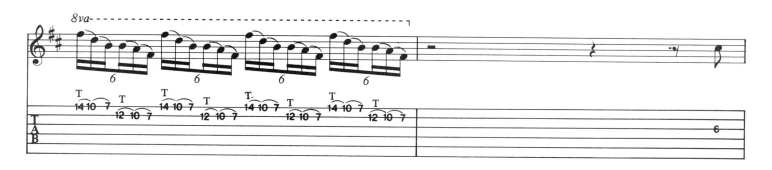

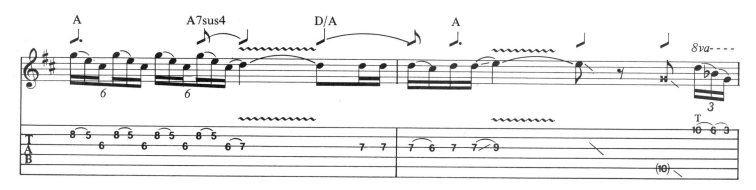

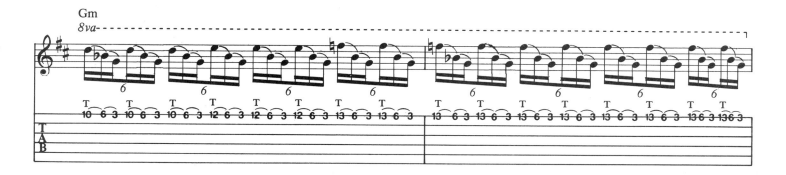

with Rhythm figures 1 and 2

Some-one send me pic-tures. Get it in the eye, take it to the Y, Spin-nin' like a

dy - na - mo.___ Feel it go-in' round and round.___

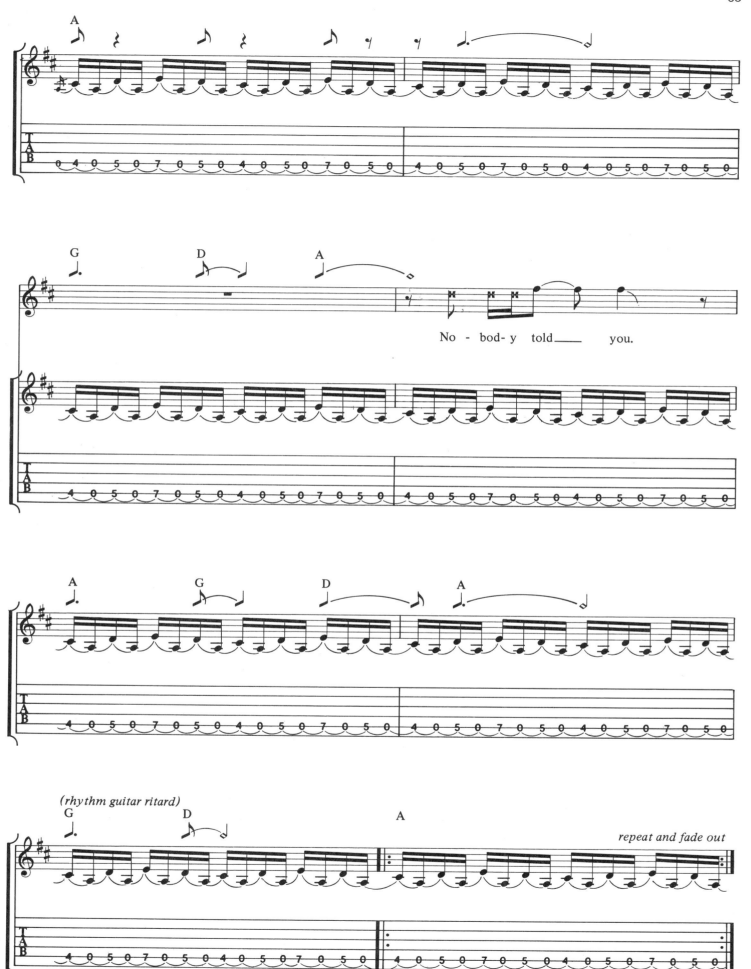

Whole Lotta Rosie

Bon Scott/Malcolm Young/Angus Young

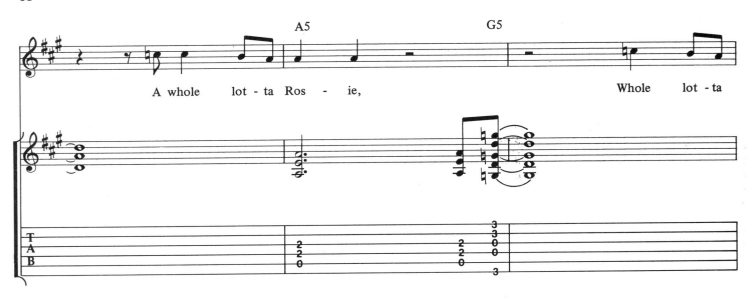

A whole lot-ta Ros - ie, Whole lot-ta

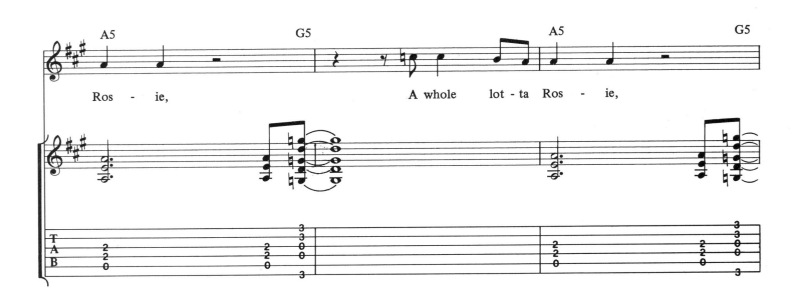

Ros - ie, A whole lot-ta Ros - ie,

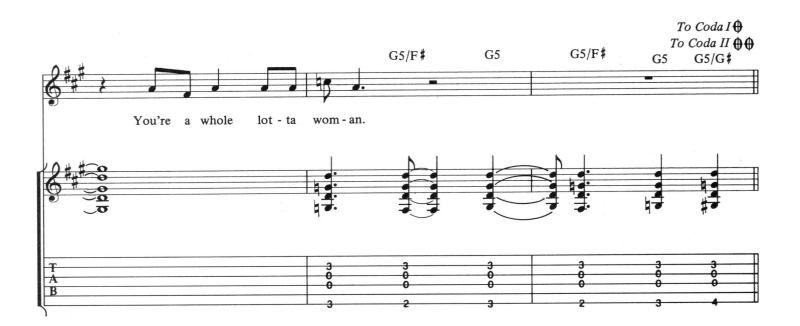

You're a whole lot-ta wom-an.

with Rhythm figure 2 (7 times)

Hon - ey you can do it,   Do it to me all night   long.—

On - ly one who turns,   On - ly one who turns   me on.—

—   All   through   the   night -

- time,   Right   a - round   the   clock,—

D.S. al Coda I

To   my   sur - prise,   Huh!—   Ros - ie nev - er stops.

Coda I

Guitar solo
A5

with Rhythm figure 2 (7 times)

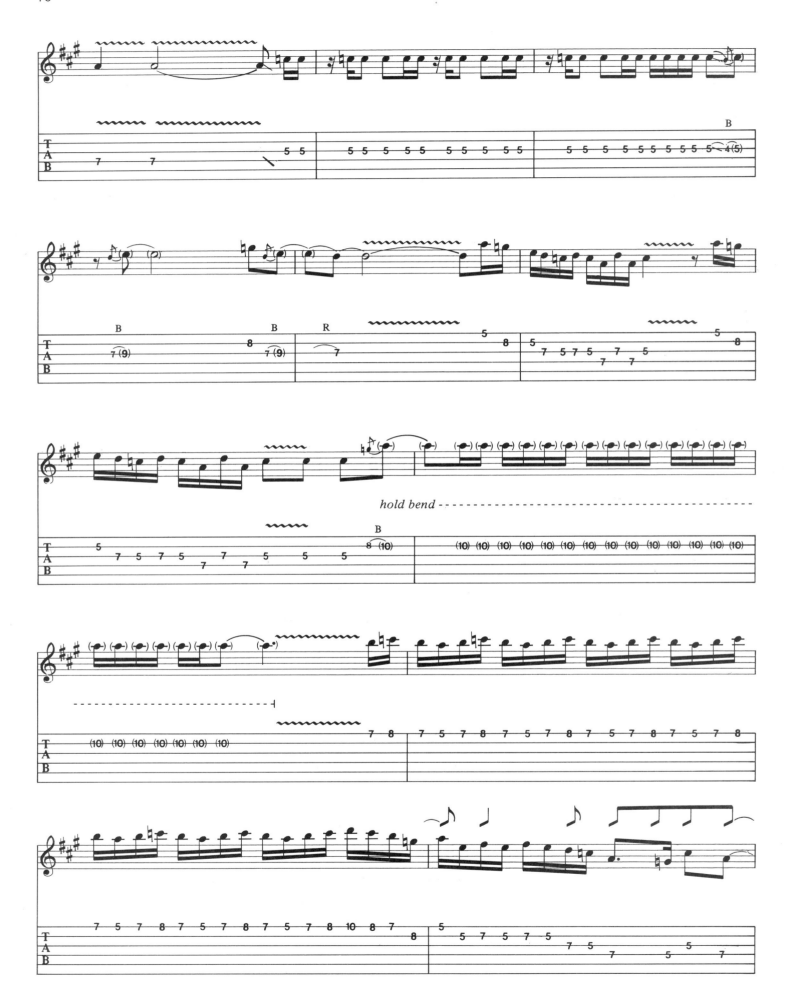

Rock n' Roll Damnation

Ronald Scott/Malcolm Young/Angus Young

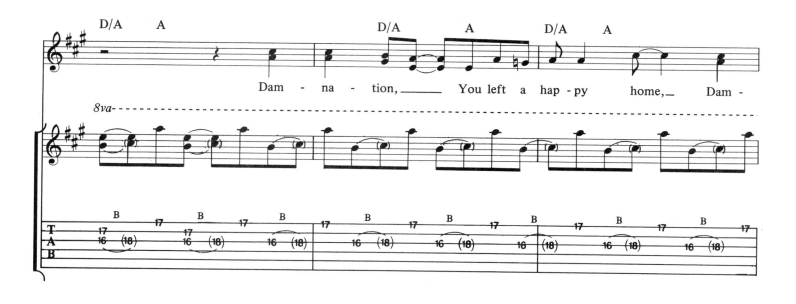

What Do You Do For Money Honey

Angus Young/Malcolm Young/Brian Johnson

What-a ya do for mon-ey hon-ey, How do you get ___ your licks? Go!

rhythm guitar

Rhythm figure 6

Guitar solo

end Rhythm figure 6

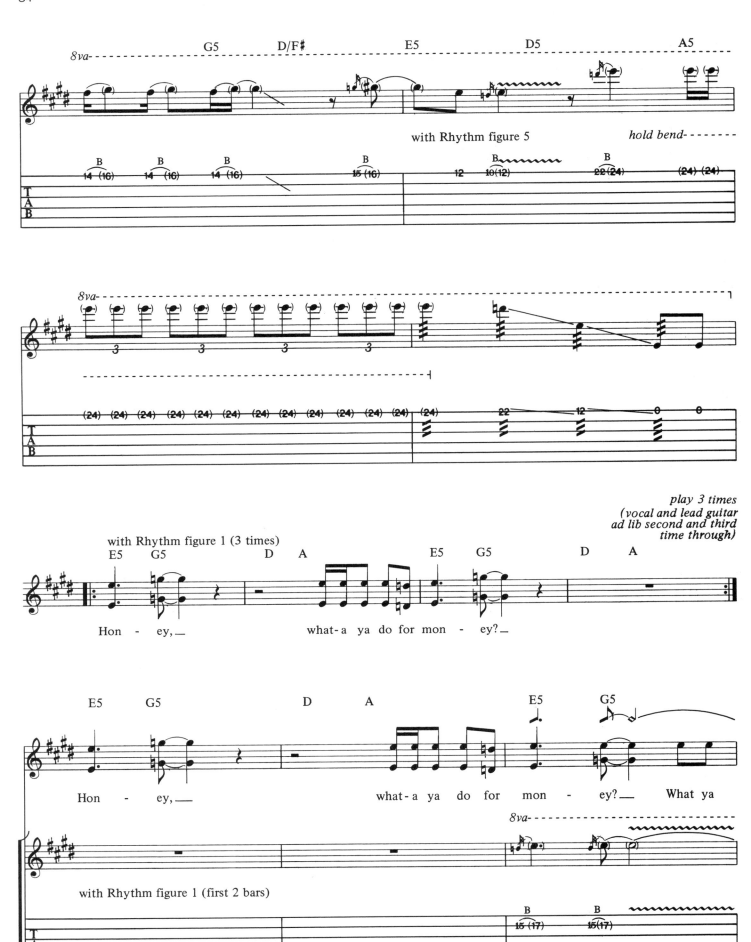

Additional Lyrics

2. You're lovin' on the take, and you're always on the make,
Squeezin' all the blood outta men.
They're standin' in a queue, just to spend a night with you;
It's business as usual again.
You're always grabbin', stabbin', try'n' to get it back in.
But girl, you must be gettin' slow,
So stop your love on the road.
All your diggin' for gold,
You make me wonder,
Yes, I wonder, I wonder.

Let There Be Rock

Ronald Scott/Angus Young/Malcolm Young

gon - na do, _ But Tchai-kov - sky had _ the news. _ He said "Let there be sound,"

And there was sound. "Let there be light,"

And there was light. "Let there be drums,"

'N' there was drums. "Let there be gui -

tar," There was gui - tar. Let there be rock. _

(vocal tacet on repeat)

Rhythm figure 2   end Rhythm figure 2

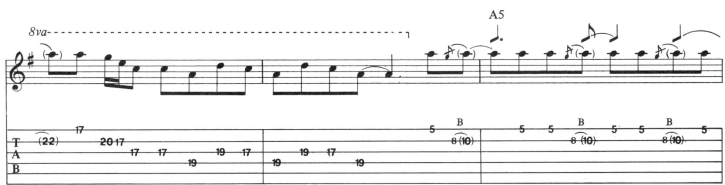

And it came to pass, That Rock 'n' Roll was born. All a-
cross the land ev-'ry rock-in' band, Was blow-in' up a storm. And the
gui-tar man got fa-mous, The busi-ness-man got rich. And in
ev-'ry bar there was a su-per-star, With a se-ven year itch.
There were fif-ty mil-lion fin-gers,
Learn-in' how to play. And you could hear the fin-gers pick-in',

High Voltage

Ronald Scott/Angus Young/Malcolm Young

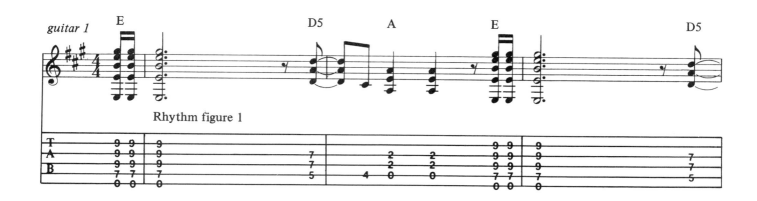

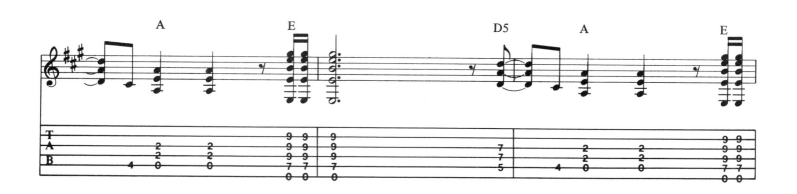

Flick Of The Switch

Brian Johnson/Angus Young/Malcolm Young

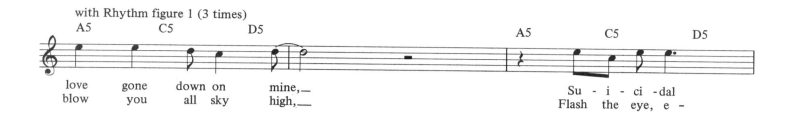

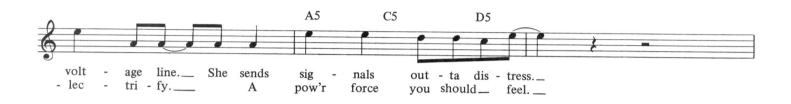

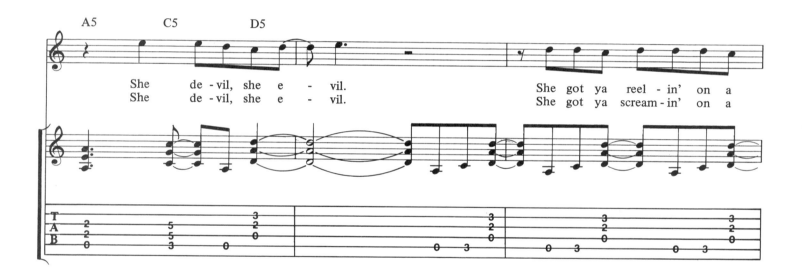

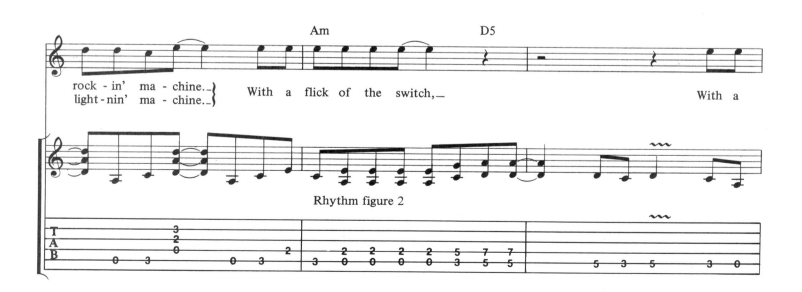

flick of the switch,__ She blow__ ya sky high. With a flick of the switch,__

end Rhythm figure 2   with Rhythm figure 2 (first 2 bars)

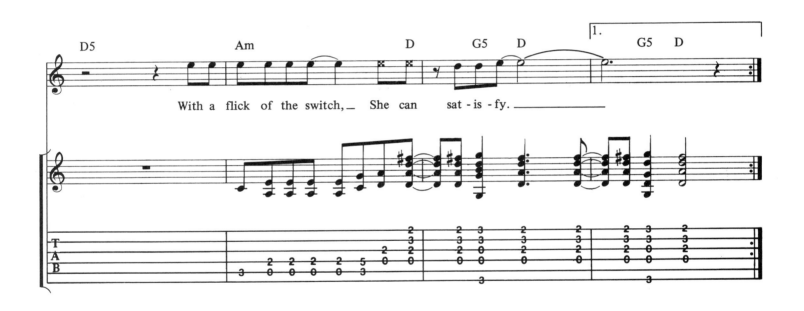

With a flick of the switch,__ She can sat - is - fy. _____

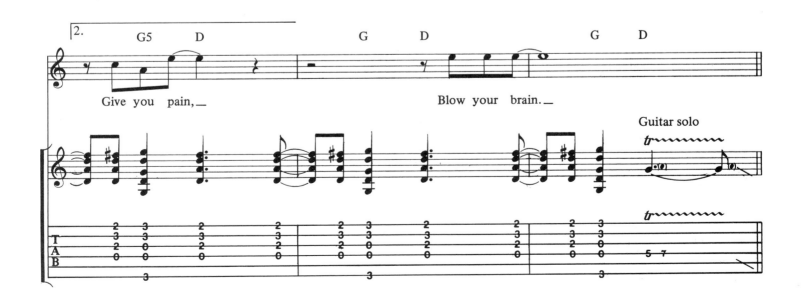

Give you pain,__   Blow your brain.__

Guitar solo

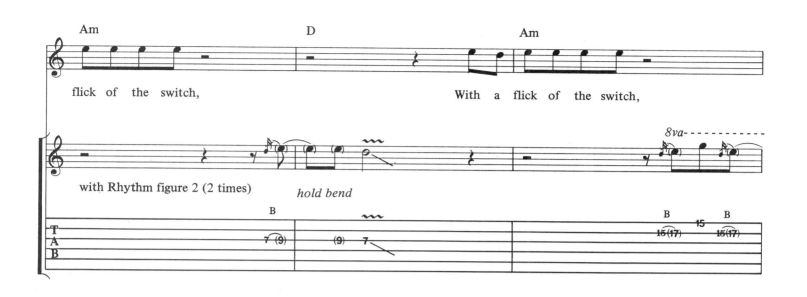

flick of the switch,   With a flick of the switch,

with Rhythm figure 2 (2 times)   *hold bend*

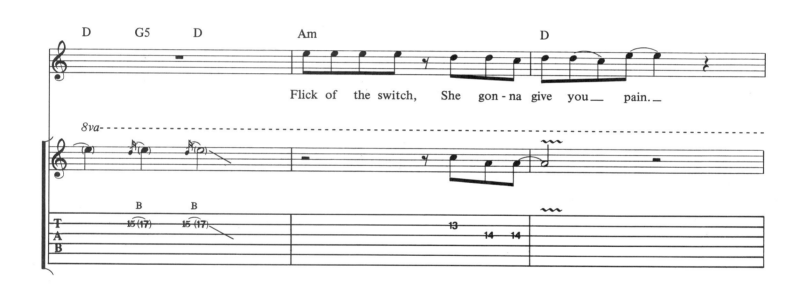

Flick of the switch, She gon-na give you__ pain.__

Flick of the switch, She's gon-na blow your brain._____

Blow your brain.

She's gon-na put the

lights out on you.

The Jack

Ronald Scott/Angus Young/Malcolm Young

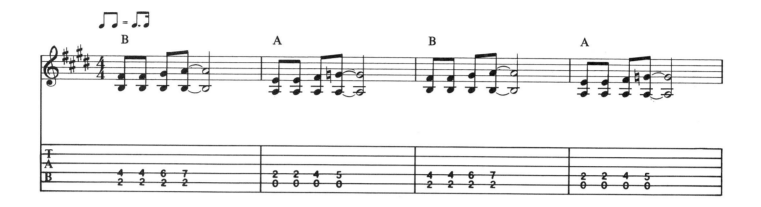

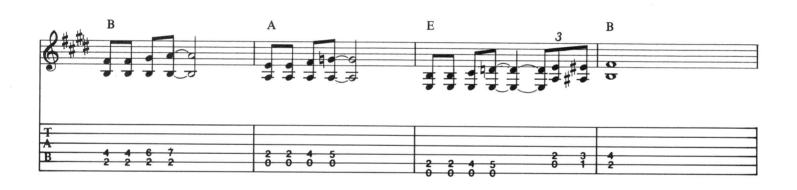

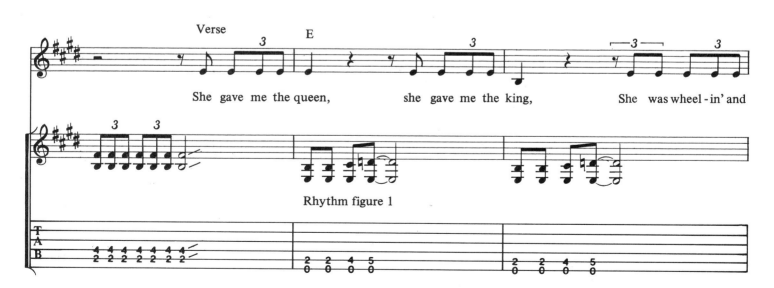

nev - er had a full house, ____ but I should have known, From the

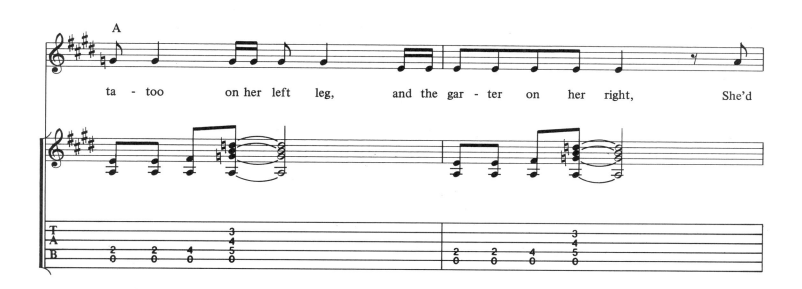

ta - too on her left leg, and the gar - ter on her right, She'd

have the card to bring me down if she played it right, She's got the

end Rhythm figure 1

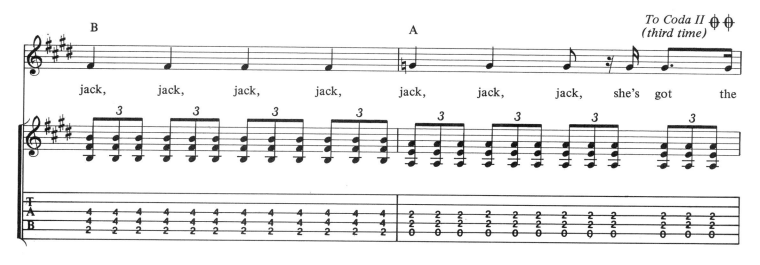

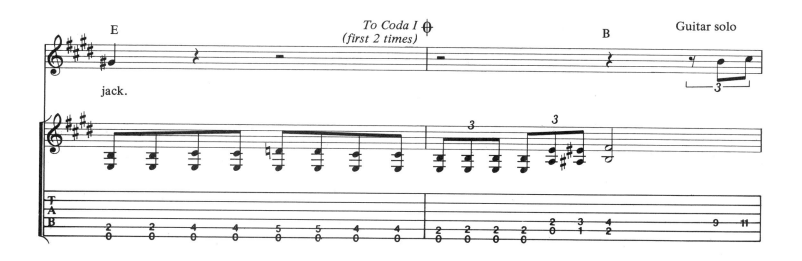

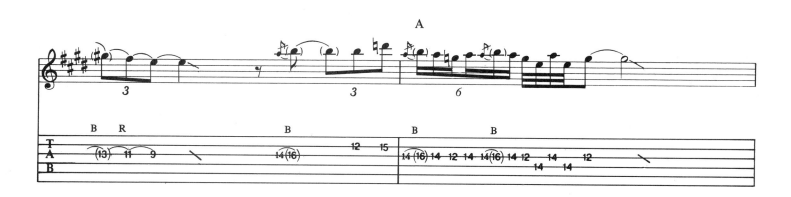

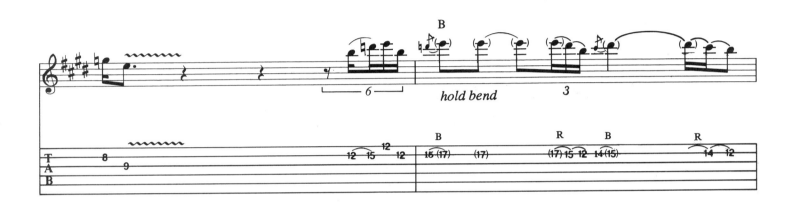

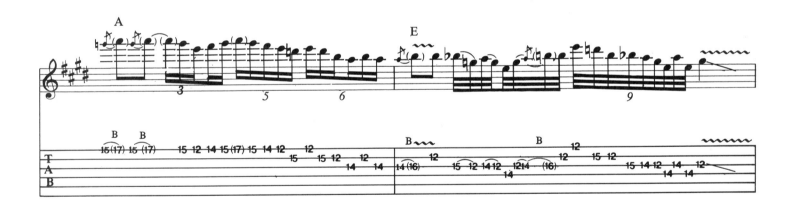

Pok - er face was her name,   pok - er face was her

na - ture, Pok - er straight was her game, if she knew she could get you. She played 'em

fast, and she played 'em hard, She could close her eyes, and feel ev -'ry

card. But how was I to know, that she'd been shuf - fled be - fore,— Said she'd

nev - er had a roy - al flush, but I should have known, That

all the cards were com - in', from the bot - tom of the pack, And if I'd

D.S. al Coda I

known what she was deal - in' out, I'd have dealt it back. She's got the

Coda I

*play chorus 3 times
(take Coda II third time)*

She's got the

Coda II

jack.

ritard

Rock n' Roll Ain't Noise Pollution

Angus Young/Malcolm Young/Brian Johnson

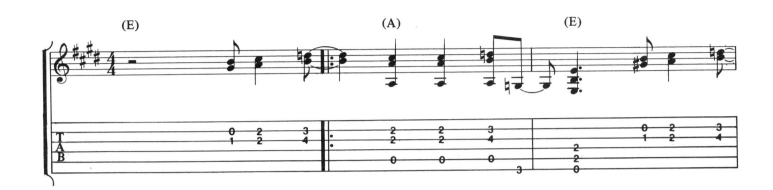

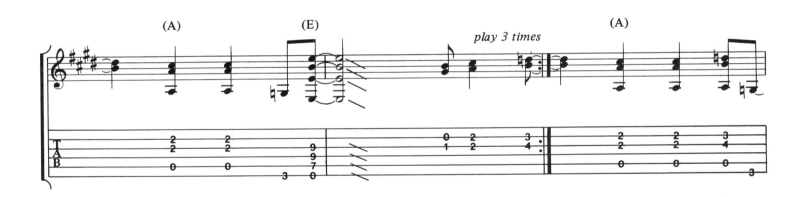

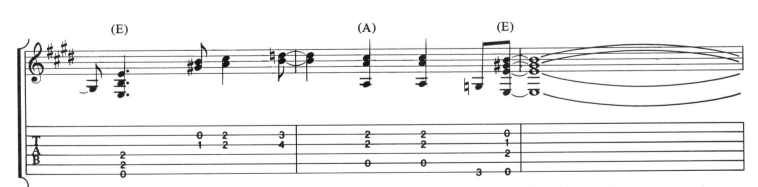

Spoken: Hey, there, all you middle men. Throw away your fancy clothes. And while you're out there sittin' on a fence, so get off your ass and come down here, 'cause rock 'n' roll ain't no riddle, man. To me it makes good, good sense.

Rhythm figure 1

end Rhythm figure 1

1. Hea - vy de - ci - bels are play - in' on my gui - tar.__ We got vi - bra - tions com - in' up from the floor.__

Rhythm figure 2

Well, just list - 'nin' to the rock that's giv - in' too much noise. Are you

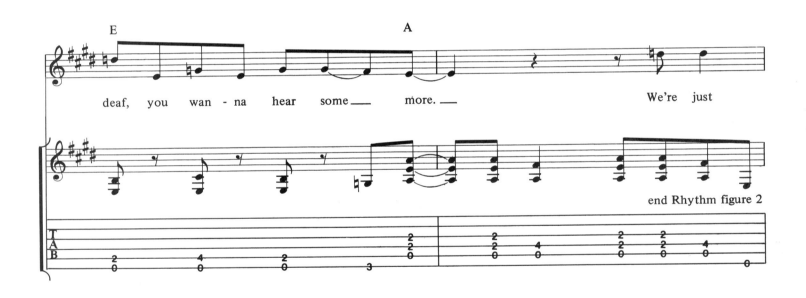

deaf, you wan - na hear some more. We're just

end Rhythm figure 2

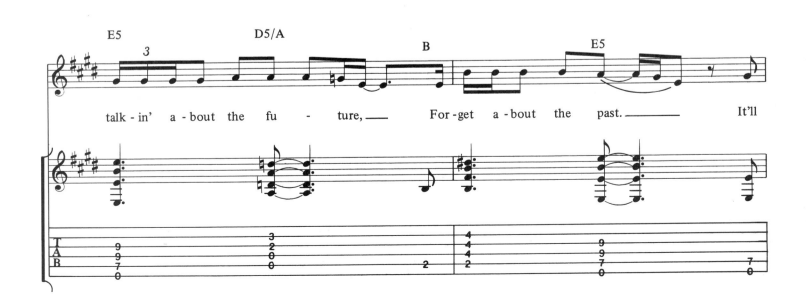

talk - in' a - bout the fu - ture, For - get a - bout the past. It'll

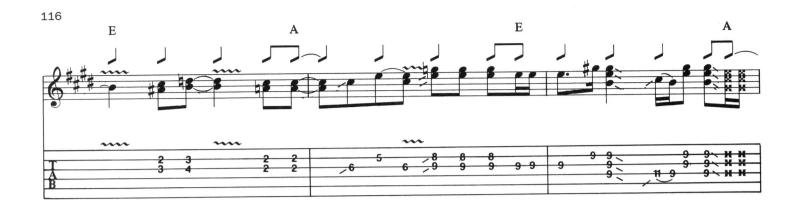

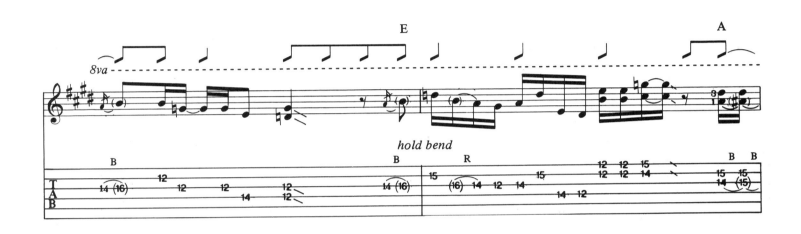

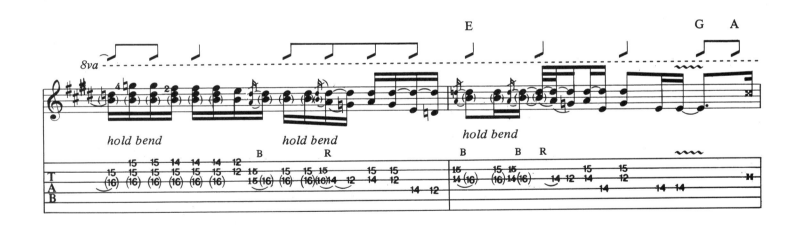

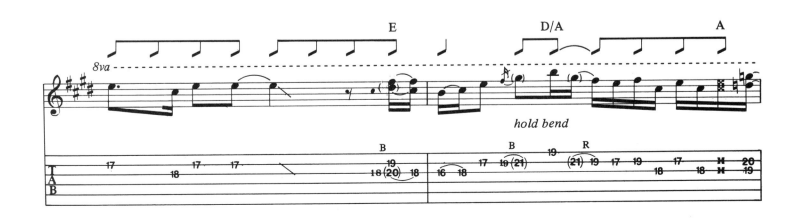

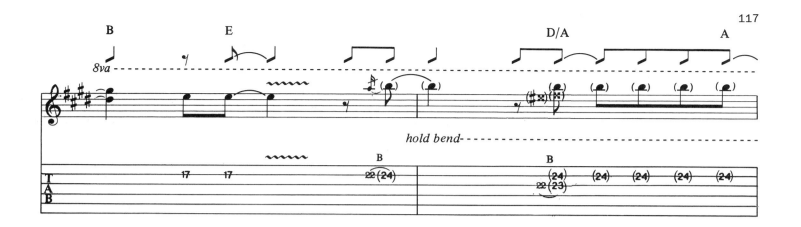

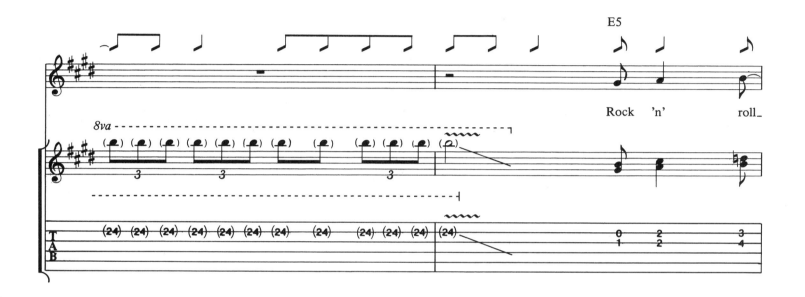

with Rhythm figure 1 (first 4 bars) (3 times)
ad lib guitar solo (16 bars)

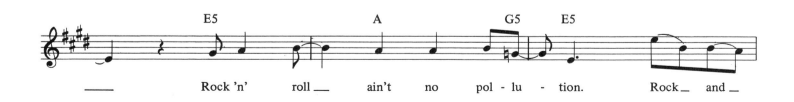

ain't noise pol-lu-tion. Rock 'n' roll ain't gon-na die.

Rock 'n' roll ain't no pol-lu-tion. Rock and

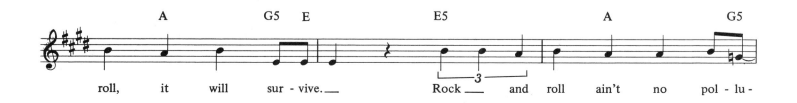

roll, it will sur-vive. Rock and roll ain't no pol-lu-

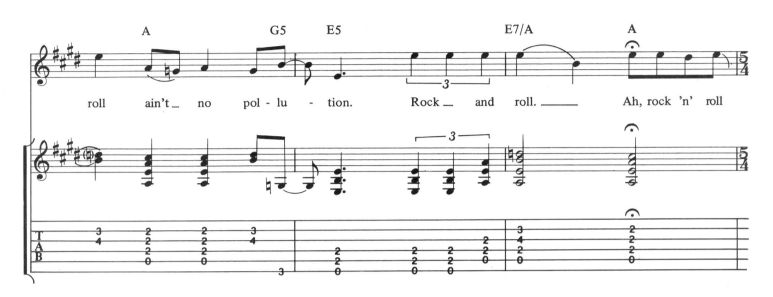

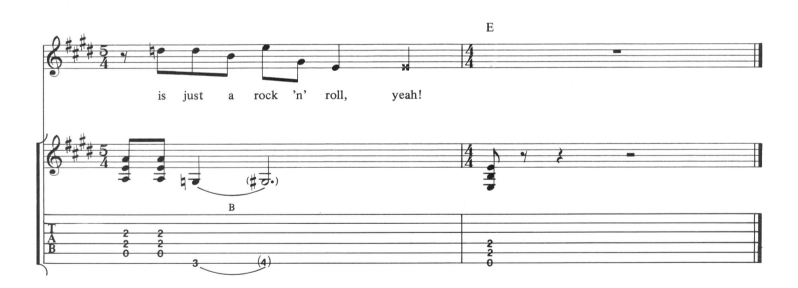

Additional Lyrics

2. I took a look inside your bedroom door,
   You looked so good lyin' on your bed.
   Well, I asked you if you wanted any rhythm and love,
   You said you wanna rock 'n' roll instead.
   We're just talkin' about the future,
   Forget about the past,
   It'll always be with us,
   It's never gonna die, never gonna die.

Dirty Deeds Done Dirt Cheap

Bon Scott/Malcolm Young/Angus Young

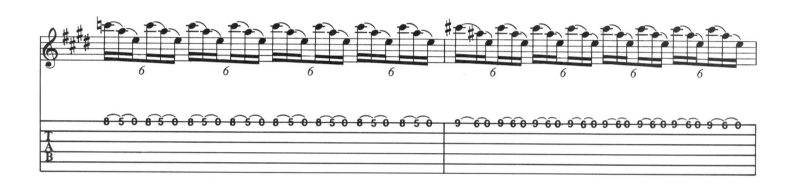

with Rhythm figure 1 (first 3 bars)

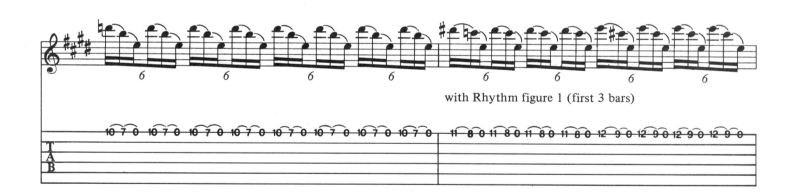

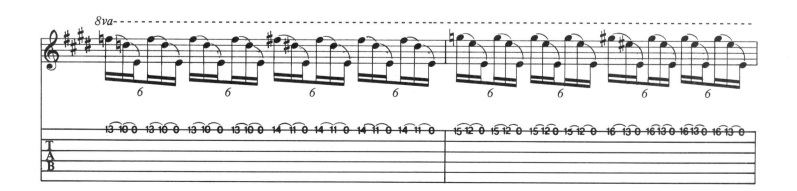

124

For Those About To Rock (We Salute You)

Angus Young/Malcolm Young/Brian Johnson

Guitar solo